MW01528988

Anderson Cooper:
A Short Biography

Crystal Reynolds

CONTENTS

1 INTRODUCTION

Star journalist and News Anchor, Anderson Hays Cooper popularly known as the witty host of the Anderson Cooper 360°, a one-hour newscast on day's top stories on Cable News Network (CNN) and contributor to CBS News' 60 Minutes. Cooper is renowned as one of the most pre-eminent newsmen, reporting all major news events around the world often from the scene itself. Earlier, Cooper has worked for ABC and served as a War correspondent in the trenches of war in Bosnia, Iran, Israel, Russia, Rwanda, Somalia, South Africa and Vietnam.

With his boyish face, steel blue eyes, premature gray-white hair and golden voice, the 48 year old is a handsome and popular TV personality and has millions of fans among both genders. His Facebook page has over 78000 likes and Twitter account is followed by nearly 7.4 million fans. A humble man, Cooper says he doesn't think too much about his status as a celebrity.

His remarkable reporting style has earned him national acclaim. He goes beyond just the headlines. When he is reporting, he's just being himself. The most appealing quality about his reporting is that he asks the questions which people would like answered. People are bound to think of him as a regular person that one can trust talking to. He is so passionate about storytelling that it absolutely infectious.

For his age, he is a physically fit man and likes to keep himself in shape. The early demise of his father due to a heart disease has taught him a lesson. He is very particular with getting his heart checked regularly, along with cholesterol and stress levels. Working out and cycles of regular exercise are a part of his daily routine followed by long stretches spent travelling, when he isn't able to work out at all. Cooper is also particular about his diet; follows a similar pattern and keeps it under control. His job often lands him in places where the food may not be easy to digest and usually he carries with him Power Bars and canned tuna.

Named as one of the Sexiest Men Alive in 2005 by People magazine, he is sometimes also called the "Silver Fox" because of his gray-white hair. At the age of 20, Cooper had started getting gray hair and by the time he was 35, it was completely gray. In his own words, "Going gray is like ejaculating: you know it can happen prematurely, but when it does it comes as a total shock."

Along with being an extraordinary news anchor, usually dressed in tailored suits, Cooper is also a fashion icon. He was among the Top 10 men on magazine Vanity Fair's international best-dressed list twice in the April 2004 issue as well as magazine's September 2006 issue.

Cooper is very fond of dogs. He called himself "total dog person" in a behind-the-scenes "60 Minutes" video in 2014.

One interesting thing that he remembers dog researcher Brian Hare telling him was, 'When dogs are looking at you, they're hugging you with their eyes,". He recently posted a picture of his new Welsh springer spaniel pup, Lilly to Instagram. Before Lily, for years he had another adorable dog Molly, also a Welsh springer spaniel who passed away in September 2015. He is also known to be great fan of the New York-based pop band Scissor Sisters.

2 CHILDHOOD

Anderson Cooper was the younger son of Wyatt Cooper (writer and editor) and Gloria Vanderbilt (an entrepreneur and jeans designer). He was born on 3rd June, 1967 at the New York City, New York, U.S. He has ancestors of various origins English, and small amounts of Dutch, Scots-Irish (Northern Irish), and Welsh, ancestry, as well as a Chilean matrilineal great-great-grandmother (who was of Spanish and Indigenous descent).

Photograph of Anderson's (left) mother Gloria and father Wyatt Cooper with elder brother Carter, at their Southampton, New York home.

Born as a brown- haired boy, Cooper came under the spotlight since very early in life. For child Anderson experience of camera, Television and media began as early as three years of age. His baby photograph taken by renowned Diane Arbus appeared on 'Harper's Bazaar'. He appeared as a guest with his heiress and jeans designer mother on 'The Tonight Show' Starring Johnny Carson in 1970 as a three year old. Again he got TV exposure as he appeared on 'To Tell the Truth as an impostor' at nine years of age. He also got a chance to model with Ford Models for Ralph Lauren, Calvin Klein when he was 10 years of age.

Though, he modelled quite a bit, he never pursued it later as a teen. In an interview to Howard Stern in 2014, he revealed the reason he had quit modelling at 13 years of age. Cooper has frequently discussed his child modelling days, but he never talked about the disturbing experience that brought about an end to this brief career.

Cooper said, "I got propositioned by a photographer...a male. He somehow got my number and called me up and offered me money, and it so freaked me out. I never told anybody. I just stopped. I was like, 'Forget it'". For the 13 years old boy, physical intimacy wasn't anything to think about. He thought the photographer was probably gay or probably that he saw that Cooper was on his own and didn't have a parent or guardian there.

He remembers how as a small boy his mother took him to look at the statue of his great-great-great-grandfather Cornelius Vanderbilt at Grand Central Station as told by him in his memoir, "Dispatches from the Edge: A Memoir of War, Disasters, and Survival". This left a deep impression in his mind. For a long time, he thought when one's older relatives died, they turned into statues. Cornelius Vanderbilt was business magnate of the Vanderbilt shipping and railroad. He made a prominent part of his vast fortune in the railroad business, which is why his statue stands at Grand Central.

As a child, he suffered from mild dyslexia as mentioned by him to Oprah Winfrey. He had a problem reading and would see some letters backward. He was coached by a special reading instructor who encouraged him to read books that he was really passionate about. The novel, "Heart of Darkness" in particular, holds his deep interest and inspires him to see "what happens to society when everything is stripped away, when you're living without the niceties of modern culture".

The top readings in Cooper's bookshelf are definitely evocative memoirs—diaries of sobriety and war, remarkable reminiscences from his own parents and a few of the classic modern novels. Most boys grow up in homes where sports are given sole importance. Commenting on his upbringing Cooper said that the home he grew up in gave great importance and value to reading and writing. As a matter of fact, even the grown up Anderson Cooper's does not have sports on his mind. Even though Anderson Cooper is a man of many interests, he admits that sports have never been his forte.

Emphasizing on his love for survival related books he was quoted, "I don't think it's an accident that I became a war correspondent. I'm interested in stories of survival: how some people make it through desperate times and others don't. If you go to a conflict zone, you find there's never a complete vacuum. There's always some form of authority. It may not make sense, and it's terrifying. You learn that people are capable of horrific brutality but also great kindness. You see things straight out of Conrad—and how a novel from the 1890s still resonates today".

In his younger days, he would often ask adults around him he respected the most, about how they succeeded to get where they were. Apparently none of them had a pre-defined, pre-planned or plotted course they could have predicted. This taught him a lesson that planning too long term may probably turn out to be a complete waste of time. The adult man has thus, since then always followed his own instincts.

In another instance he recalls how as a child, he loved to spend summers running along the edge of the sand cliffs at the beach. In his own words, "As I ran, I could feel the sand collapse beneath me, but as long as I kept moving forward, kept running fast, I could stay one step ahead of the falling cliff. That's what anchoring the news is like. You can easily falter; easily destroy your career in a sentence or two. The key is to keep going, keep moving and never forget you're running on sand."

As perceived by others Cooper's childhood looked perfect. The world outside believed that Cooper had a life of privilege, child born with a golden spoon, growing up in Manhattan's wealthiest neighborhoods as the son of heiress and successful fashion jeans designer Gloria Vanderbilt. Being son to famous socialite and jeans designer, people were subjected to think of his life as rich, wealthy and happy but the reality was very different. In an interview he told Brad Goldfarb in a candid comment, "Certainly, growing up, there was a nice apartment and nice things in the apartment, but for me, one of the greatest privileges of my background was realizing that what a lot of people think they want will not ultimately make them happier."

Cooper was just merely 10 years old when his father died unexpectedly during heart surgery. This is one of the toughest ages to lose a parent. Cooper cherishes memories of his father, who had lived in the Big Easy as a teenager. When he was a child, his father would often take him there for visits. For a 10 year boy, it was difficult to cope with the grief. His father's death affected him a lot and he closed himself off to the world. This turning point for him grew inside him the desire to become absolutely self-reliant.

3 EDUCATION

Cooper's did his education from the Dalton School, a private co-educational university preparatory day school in Manhattan. The decision was primarily taken by his mother because she was of the opinion that its emphasis on the arts over athletics would provide a firmer grounding for Anderson.

As a 10 year old boy, Cooper suffered grief due to his father's early demise. He tried to deal with this loss by cutting up with the rest of the world. He became more determined to stand on his own feet and become self-reliant. Wanting to stay prepared for future losses, Cooper took survivalist courses while in high school.

Cooper left school at the age of 17, in his senior year at Dalton after graduating a semester early and drove across Africa in a truck. He travelled around for several months, meaning it to be a "survival trip". Unfortunately for him during this time, he contracted malaria while there and had to be hospitalized in Kenya. Cooper always described the experience in Africa as a place to forget and be forgotten in.

Later Cooper earned degree in political science and international relations from Yale University, 1989. Talking about grades and education, he had once remarked that he has never been asked about his grades or his senior thesis at Yale. In his words, "All those things were hugely important to me at the time, but right now, in truth they are dim memories for me. When you graduate the slate is wiped clean."

As fate would have it, the 21 year old had to face another tragedy of almost unimaginable sorrow: his elder brother, Carter, committed suicide by jumping out of the 14th-floor window of their mother's New York City apartment in front of her.

After graduating from Yale, he was planning to take the U.S. Foreign Service examination, a common career choice given his Ivy-League major. He had worked as an intern for two summers at the Central Intelligence Agency. However, he was not very interested in pursuing this line of career and opted instead to become a news correspondent and journalist. Despite having received no formal educational background, he aspired to get into news reporting and journalism. His first correspondence work in the early 1990s was as a self-proclaimed reporter. After working for a brief period, he took a break and moved to Vietnam for a year where he studied the Vietnamese language at the University of Hanoi.

Later in an attempt to find a job as an on-air reporter, he repeatedly tried gaining entry-level employment with American Broadcasting Company (ABC) answering telephones, but was unsuccessful. Not discouraged in the least, a self-made man, he became a self-taught journalist.

With the help of a friend, he entered Myanmar with a fake press pass and made his own news coverage which he sold to a small Channel One.

4 FAMILY LIFE

Anderson Cooper was born to people coming from two contrasting economic backgrounds. His mother Gloria Vanderbilt, artist, jeans designer and heiress belonged to the richest families in America and his father, writer and editor Wyatt Cooper, came from a family in Mississippi with no money. Millionaire equestrian Reginald Claypoole Vanderbilt and socialite Gloria Morgan Vanderbilt were his maternal grandparents and his maternal great-great-great-grandfather was business magnate Cornelius Vanderbilt.

He is also a descendant, through his mother, of Civil War brevet Major General Hugh Judson Kilpatrick, who was with General William T. Sherman on his march through

Georgia. Through his "Vanderbilt" line, he is a second cousin, once removed, of screenwriter James Vanderbilt. Also he is the third cousin once removed of Timothy Olyphant.

Cooper has two older half-brothers from his mother's marriage to music conductor Leopold Stokowski, Leopold Stanislaus "Stan" Stokowski (1950) and Christopher Stokowski (1952). Cooper is also uncle to two half-nieces and one half-nephew by his elder half-brother Stan Stokowski: Aurora (born March 1983), Abra (born 1985) and Myles (born 1998).

In 2014, Cooper appeared in Henry Louis Gates' Finding Your Roots, where he found out about an ancestor, Burwell Boykin, who was a slave owner from the South.

5 RELATIONSHIP WITH HIS MOTHER

Cooper shares a very special relationship with his mother. After the loss of his father at the age of 10, he only had one parent. He describes her as the most vulnerable and optimistic person he knows. He believes while his mother is the most trusting person, he himself is not as trusting as her. She may be full of incredible optimism; he is often the one procrastinating about the next catastrophe right around the corner.

Anderson Cooper's mother is the great-great-granddaughter of shipping and railroad business magnate Cornelius Vanderbilt, who died in 1877. Apparently she is the sole heiress to a fortune estimated at $200 million left by

Cornelius. As a young woman, Gloria had a glittering social life and became very popular as a designer to her own jeans brand.

Her many romantic relationships often headlined the newspapers. Her fascination with Hollywood led her to marry Errol Flynn when she was 17. After the short-lived marriage, she married famous conductor Leopold Stokowski when she was 20 and he was 63 producing two children Christopher Stokowski and Leopold Stanislaus Stokowski. This marriage too ended followed by a vicious and well-publicized custody battle of her boys, then aged three and five.

Afterwards she married director Sidney Lumet and then writer Wyatt Cooper. The final and fourth marriage to Cooper, finally brought Gloria the happiness and joy of family she'd craved her entire life. Cooper's parents were married on Christmas Eve of 1963 and his mother was soon expecting his elder brother Carter and then himself. She doted on her younger son and has dedicated her book,

A Mother's Story, to him.

Despite being the descendent of America's business tycoon Cornelius Vanderbilt, he never felt much of a part of his mother's family. The surname "Vanderbilt" never had any reality to him. He did not want it to be a baggage with him and presumed that he would use the name to his advantage. He even remarked that his mother didn't feel connected to her family either. With a mother who was not much of a part in her growing up and no father, his mother Gloria felt more of an impostor.

In 1988, Cooper and his mother went through an ultimate nightmare with the loss of his elder brother Carter. His brother just after his graduation from Princeton, Carter jumped out the window of the 14th floor of his mother's. Vanderbilt says in the HBO documentary "Nothing Left Unsaid" that she contemplated following him, but the thought of how it would devastate Anderson stopped her.

With a woman of incredible resilience and strength,

Cooper has always looked up to his mother. He overwhelmed with the tragedy and the past, remembers his mother was so shattered that she basically went to bed for three weeks and just cried.

Cooper wasn't as close with his mother as he wanted to be. He hardly knew anything about his mother's childhood because Gloria had never spoken to him about it. A documentary, "Nothing Left Unsaid" that went on air on 9th April 2016 on HBO at 9pm, featuring Cooper and his mother Gloria, is a series of candid conversations about themselves, their family, and the relationship between mother and son. The documentary brought him and his mother together, since they really got to know each other and became really close in a way that they never had been before.

6 FATHER'S LOSS

Cooper's father Wyatt Cooper died during open heart surgery on Jan. 5, 1978, at the age of 50. At the time, Cooper was only 10 years old. He opened about the effect of his father's death on him on his CNN segment. He believes that the death of loved ones has changed him. His father's loss affected him, particularly since he was devoid of a parent at a young age. He suddenly felt that the world seemed a much different and more dangerous place. He was devastated to that point that he completely closed himself off the outside world.

Cooper sometimes regrets that he had reacted in that way. The person he was before his father's death and the he meant to be was far more open and more interesting than the person he had become. But the tragic incident made him determined to become self-reliant and independent and brought out the best in him.

He has dedicated a part of a series of stories called "The Person Who Changed My Life" to his late father. He wrote, "He gave me the sense that I had value, that my ideas mattered," "That instilled in me a confidence I don't think I would have otherwise had." Cooper had also written about his father in his memoir, "Dispatches from the Edge: A Memoir of War, Disasters, and Survival" in 2006, where he described the experience of losing both a parent and a brother to early deaths. "I used to think that was old, but now that I'm 48, 50 seems pretty young," Cooper said.

He remembers the joy of being brought up by both of his parents. For a growing child the love of a parent is the basis of a foundation that can carry him through all sorts of good and bad, ups and downs in life. He feels lucky enough to still carry the feelings of security and confidence with him today.

The suffering of his father due to a heart disease made him realize the importance of staying fit and healthy. Without fail, he carries out his daily routine of exercise and working out and complete control on his diet intake.

7 BROTHER'S SUICIDE

The suicide of Carter Cooper in 1988, the 23-year-old son of socialite and jeans designer Gloria Vanderbilt came as a huge shock to the people in their society circles. The tragic loss to Gloria and 21 year old Anderson seemed to touch families everywhere.

Cooper's elder brother and only sibling, Carter, died after committing suicide by jumping from the family's 14th-floor balcony window. The combined loss of his father and elder brother shattered Cooper and left him numb with grief and pain. He never talked about what he went through after this happened, not even with his mother. Instead, he the only escape to drown out his own grief was by reporting on the tragic losses of others.

A month prior to his death, Carter had started seeing a therapist for depression. Cooper's mother wrote about the death in her book A Mother's Story, in which she expresses her belief that Carter's suicide was the result of psychotic episode followed by an allergy to the anti-asthma prescription drug salbutamol.

While Carter's suicide came as a big blow to him, Cooper feels that it ignited his interest in journalism and news reporting. After his brother sudden death, he often thought of loss as a theme and connected it to his work. He feels since he had experienced loss in his life he dwelled on questions about survival. Cooper wondered why few people were able to thrive in situation, while few others could not tolerate those situations. He did not if he would be able to survive and felt confused on how to get on in the world on his own, without the support of a father or elder brother.

He had once mentioned to Howard Stern on his Sirius

radio show that Carter's suicidal jump from the window of their mother's 14th-floor Manhattan apartment is something he cannot forget and still thinks about it every day. Even if it is not the first thing he thinks of in the morning, but since years together there's not been a single day, that goes by without thinking of his brother.

Going further on the tragic incident, Cooper believes that it still shapes his life. He admits Carter was so much smarter than him. Carter graduated from Princeton and landed himself a good job at the American Heritage as a book editor. Thinking back at that time, the realization that his brother had committed suicide was inconceivable for him.

Cooper also admitted that after the tragedy, he was certainly worried about following similar dark tendencies that might be buried deep inside him. When Carter jumped out of the window to his death, their mother was right there in the house. But Cooper never blamed her for it.

Recalling what happened that day, Cooper said Carter

had just woken up from a nap and was disoriented and ran to mother's room and said, 'What's going on, what's going on?' Then he ran back to his room and went out onto the ledge. Cooper thinks of the situation as an impulse that his brother could not contain. An examination conducted later showed that there were no traces of drugs or alcohol found in Carter's system. Cooper says that to this day, the family still doesn't understand why he did it.

"With suicide," said Cooper, "we like to think that it's this clear thing, and it's not – and that's the horrible thing about suicide. The family members are left for their entire lives wondering why. Sometimes there isn't any why."

8 RELATIONSHIP WITH HALF-BROTHERS

Anderson Cooper has two half-brothers, Stan and Chris Stokowski from his mother's marriage to the famous conductor Leopold Stokowski. Some 40 years back, Cooper had been very close to his half-brother Chris, who was 15 years elder to him. Chris had vanished after cutting himself off from the clan. Cooper confesses that he has not been in touch with his half-brother since then.

As a child Chris was quite shy, aloof and had a solitary life as a student at Bard College. He did not take his mother's fame and popularity as a jeans designer in a good stride. He also usually refrained from using his surname as he believed in making his own career as a musician.

The reason behind his sudden disappearance was supposedly a bizarre dispute over their mother Gloria Vanderbilt's therapist as revealed by MailOnline. Chris severed all relationships with his family and became a recluse after his mother's therapist interfered in his love life. He had stopped speaking to his mom after her therapist at the time, Dr. Zois, allegedly influenced Chris' relationship with his ex-fiancée.

Anderson had always adored Chris and felt heartbroken and dejected when he abandoned them. Chris, who was 15 years older than Anderson, spoiled him with Lego sets and other toys. They both spent a lot of time together as kids frequently on the beach building sand castles.

9 A HARDWORKING CAREER

Though born into a family of money, Anderson Cooper was clear about his goals, since he was a 10 year old. He wanted to earn his own money, become self-dependent and self-reliant. Cooper started his career early in life just as a young boy. He got his first pay by modelling with Ford Models for Ralph Lauren, Calvin Klein when he was 10 years old. However after this brief career, he did not pursue it quit later. As a teenager, he took a job as a waiter in the summers. He waited at the Mortimer's, a famous eating joint at Manhattan frequently visited by Park Avenue society types.

After graduating from Yale, he did internship for two

summers at the Central Intelligence Agency (CIA). But not really interested in this field, he moved on to pursue his dream of news reporting and journalism.

After graduating, his first job was of a fact checker in 1989 for the small news network Channel One. This channel broadcast daily youth-oriented news program to many classrooms in junior high and high schools in the United States. This was a desk job and got boring since he was not able to get an interview at any of the major networks' news departments. Thus, he took a break and he decided to go to Vietnam to study the Vietnam language, and took a video camera with him.

Even though Cooper had no formal educational training in journalism, he was persistent to find a job of his interest. He obtained a fake press pass and credentials a friend had made for him on a computer. With this pass, he entered Myanmar on his own and met with students fighting the national Burmese government. There he managed to film some footage about that country's internal strife.

He became a self-taught journalist and sold the news coverage that he made on his own to a Channel One. Cooper then lived in Vietnam to study the Vietnamese language for a year at the University of Hanoi. He took permission from Channel One to allow him to bring his Hi-8 camera along, so that he could shoot and film reports of Vietnamese life and culture to would then be aired on Channel One. Later some time, he went back to Africa, and filed stories for Channel One as a freelance new correspondent from 1990-93 on such topics as a spreading famine in Somalia. He was appointed as the channel's chief international correspondent by 1993. Then his job included reporting from international danger zones like the Balkans and central Africa and Cooper started attracted the attention of the major news organizations.

Talking about those days, Cooper wanted to prepare himself for future losses. This led to his becoming a freelance journalist and treading in dangerous water, travelling alone to report news stories on conflicts in faraway places like Burma and Bosnia. He often reflected on survival, both others' and his own.

He recalls one such violence torn incident when he reporting from Rwanda during the 1994 genocide. Reporting about war and blood-shed for year, Cooper had seen enough death. In Rwanda, he came across dead bodies that had been in the sun for several days. The skin of a woman's hand was peeling off like a glove. Out of habit for a news reporter, he snapped the close up picture for his personal portfolio. As he did, someone took a photo of him. Later when Cooper saw his own photo, he realized he needed to move forward from just reporting news showing war horrors.

Soon, ABC News hired Cooper for the position of a correspondent in 1995. This involved working mostly in the United States, which suited him pretty much. He had decided to give up searching the world for feeling and needed to find it closer to home. He was reporting primarily for "World News Saturday/Sunday". Eventually he rose to be promoted as the co-anchor of its overnight news broadcast program 'World News Now' in 1999. Along with anchoring ABC's live, interactive news and interview program 'World News Now', he was also providing reports for "World News Tonight," "20/20" and "20/20 Downtown." The program aired from 3 a.m. to 5 a.m. early morning and thus, Cooper had to work tirelessly overnights anchoring this newscast, along with the day program at 20/20. After a while, the schedule became irksome, tiring and arduous. He was catching sleep in two or four-hour shifts and was looking forward to a change. He wanted to clear his head and get out of news a little bit, and became was interested in reality TV.

He has been quoted saying, "There's something about doing live TV and being there as it happens that's always appealed to me. I think there's great value to bearing witness to these events as they're actually happening."

Soon he moved on to hosting ABC's reality show, 'The Mole' in 2000 which is a competition consisting of contestants who work together to add money to a pot that only one of them will win in the end. He left the game show after its second season. For him two seasons was enough and he thought he needed to be getting back to news.

By this time, Cooper's popularity as a TV personality was growing. Talking about Cooper's working style, producer David Perozzi of ABC News had remarked that he was really intense where his job is concerned. He could not care less how he looks, his hair and makeup. If there's no cameraperson, he grabs the camera. He's just as human as all.

With the devastating Twin tower attack on the World Trade Center and Pentagon in September 11, 2001, Cooper was ready to make a comeback to reporting of hard news. He was lucky enough to be hired by CNN in January of 2002 as a correspondent and substitute anchor.

Initially he returned to broadcast news in 2001, anchored alongside Paula Zahn on 'American Morning' on CNN. Soon he was offered to anchor CNN's weekend prime-time program in 2002. Since 2002, he has hosted CNN's New

Year's Eve special from Times Square. CNN called out Cooper to take over Paula Zahn's two-hour nightly newscast and this made him a huge success among viewers. With his higher ratings, he finally got his own newscast. Zahn covered in–detail news held the 8 p.m. slot, where she with Cooper leading in at the 7 p.m.

And Cooper began anchoring 'Anderson Cooper 360'in 2003, a news cast on CNN which is broadcast around the world on CNN International. The program covers a number of news stories of the day from around the world and includes analysis from experts on the highlighted issues. The show made its debut on September 8, 2003, and Cooper quickly accrued an audience for his witty, intelligent, sometimes bemused delivery of the day's top stories.

He covered several important news stories in 2005 which included the tsunami in Sri Lanka, the Cedar revolution, the death of Pope John Paul II, and the royal wedding of Prince Charles and Camilla Parker Bowles. This news coverage brought him national fame and earned him several prestigious awards.

The coverage of post-Hurricane Katrina, New Orleans by Cooper in 2005 was so electrifying that it for the first time lifted him to national prominence. During CNN coverage of the aftermath of Hurricane Katrina, Cooper's confrontation with Sen. Mary Landrieu, Sen. Trent Lott, and the Rev. Jesse Jackson about their perception of the government response made headlines.

In a live 2005 exchange with Sen. Mary Landrieu, Cooper emotionally interjected "Excuse me...to listen to politicians thanking each other and complimenting each other... there are a lot of people here who are very upset and very angry... It... cuts them the wrong way right now, because literally there was a body on the streets of this town yesterday being eaten by rats because this woman had been laying in the street for 48 hours."

Cooper had covered news for the Niger famine from Maradi in Aug 2005. He was also added as a co-anchor to the show 'NewsNight' in 2005 as a temporary arrangement. The reason for this was that the format of the show was changed from 60 to 120 minutes to cover the unusually violent hurricane season. In order to distribute some of the increased workload, Cooper was temporarily added as co-anchor to Aaron Brown. This arrangement was reported to have been made permanent the same month by the president of CNN's U.S. operations, Jonathan Klein, who has called Cooper "the anchorperson of the future. The rating for the program towered significantly with Cooper's introduction and he was made a permanent co-anchor.

To leverage on Cooper's fan following, his show 'Anderson Cooper 360' was expanded to two hours and was shifted to the 10 pm slot in November 2005 by CNN. Aaron Brown had to ultimately leave CNN, ostensibly having "mutually agreed" with Jonathan Klein on the matter since he was left with no options for him to host shows. In early 2007 Cooper signed a multi-year deal with CNN, which would allow him to continue as a contributor to 60 Minutes. CNN was pleased with Cooper's work and performance that the multi-year deal came with a doubling of his salary from $2 million annually to $4 million in 2007.

Cooper also got the golden opportunity to interview news legend Walter Cronkite at the Gibson Amphitheatre in Universal City, California, in the second installment of a four-part University of Judaism Public Lecture Series on 26th February 2007.

In July 2007, Cooper moderated the first presidential debate using YouTube technology. Cooper was also fortunate to host the acclaimed CNN series, "Planet in Peril," that was premiered in October 2007. He hosted the documentary with Sanjay Gupta and Jeff Corwin on CNN and also hosted the 'CNN Heroes: An All-Star Tribute', a show in which ordinary people who perform extraordinary deeds are honoured. Cooper was also ready to fill-in co-host for Regis Philbin for the TV talk show *Live with Regis and Kelly* in 2007 when the host had to undergo a triple-bypass heart surgery.

In 2010, Cooper had undertaken the coverage of the Gulf of Mexico oil spill; this was marked by an impassioned advocacy for that region. Completely dedicated to his job, he was the only journalist to have spent far more days in Louisiana than any other journalist.

In his first attempt in hosting a daytime talk show, he hosted 'Anderson Live', a syndicated show that debuted in September 2011 as simply 'Anderson'. The show is distributed in the U.S. and Canada by Warner Bros. Television. Warner Bros. and Telepictures (both corporate siblings of CNN) announced in September 2010 that Cooper had signed an agreement to host the nationally syndicated talk show. The show's final episode was aired in May 2013.

It was reported by The New York Times' Brian Stelter on Twitter that the new Warner Bros. daytime talk show would be named Anderson (now titled Anderson Live). As a part of negotiations over the talk show deal, Cooper also entered into another new multi-year contract with CNN to continue as the host of Anderson Cooper 360°. The announcement that

Anderson Live would end at the conclusion of its second season came on October 29, 2012. This season of the show, slightly renamed to 'Anderson Live' and revamped with a variety of co-hosts, could not gather as many ratings as distributor Warner Brothers had hoped for. The final Anderson Live aired on May 20, 2013.

Departing from the usual TV news anchoring, Cooper gave his voice as the narrator for the 2011 Broadway revival of *'How to Succeed in Business without Really Trying'*, directed by Rob Ashford and starring Harry Potter fame actor Daniel Radcliffe.

Cooper is also a prolific writer and writes a monthly column for Details magazine. He writes freelance and has authored a variety of articles that have appeared in many other outlets. In October 2005, it was announced that he signed a US $1 million contract to write a memoir for Harper Collins detailing his "life as a journalist and human being in Sri Lanka, Africa, Iraq and Louisiana/Mississippi" over the previous year. It was titled *Dispatches from the Edge: A*

Memoir of War, Disasters, and Survival and was released 23 May 2006. Some of Cooper's proceeds are being donated to charity. In addition, the book topped the New York Times bestseller list on 18 June 2006.

Another memoir, this one written with his mother, heiress and socialite Gloria Vanderbilt, released in April 2016. *The Rainbow Comes and Goes: a Mother and Son Talk about Life, Love, and Loss* was published by HarperCollins on 5th April, four days before the airing of an HBO documentary about Vanderbilt, "Nothing Left Unsaid."

Anderson Cooper has faced so many war-like zones while covering news stories that situations like dodging explosions in Gaza and braved rioters in Egypt have become a part and parcel of his life.

During the Egypt conflict in 2011, quite a few reporters on scene location trying to take the latest story on the ongoing were attacked and harmed. Anderson Cooper and his CNN crew team were no exception. Cooper were attacked and punched in the head by supporters of Egypt's president, Hosni Mubarak.

Another time in 2012, on one such assignment for CBS's 60 Minutes on a trip to Portugal, the journalist spent several hours on a boat on an overcast day and woke up later that night to discover a white patch over his right eye.

As he had spent the entire day in sun rays, the Ultra Violet (UV) light bounced off water and affected his eyes adversely leading him to be temporarily blinded. Cooper described his 36 hours of blindness during the broadcast of his CNN talk show, Anderson Live, telling viewers that he didn't know constant sun exposure could cause him to lose his eyesight. He had never really thought this would be putting himself in danger.

"I wake up in the middle of the night and it feels like my eyes are on fire — my eyeballs — and I think, oh maybe I have sand in my eyes or something," he said. "I douse my eyes with water. Anyway, it turns out I have sunburned my eyeballs and I go blind."

Even then going through the painful experience, nothing deterred the man from his job. Taking it in a good stride, the handsome News anchor remained good-humoured about the entire incident, showing several pictures of him sporting eye patches. He even posted a picture on his fan page on Instagram. And true to their star journalist, hundreds of fans wished him a speedy recovery. Jokingly he remarked the picture is his new Match.com profile picture, probably it would really work for him.

The famous news reporter and journalist find this way of tracking grief around the globe, the only solution to drowning out his own feelings of loss. While covering the news in Sri Lanka after the 2004 tsunami, in which 35,000 died and millions were left homeless, Cooper met a small group of women, each of whom had lost a loved one to the sea. Watching them talk through their pain, Cooper felt a twinge of envy for them. After several years have passed since his father and brother expired he writes in his new memoir, Dispatches from the Edge, he still does not have the ability to talk about his past. The only way he can overcome his own grief is by listening to these people. This is one of the reasons that new reporting from around the world has attracted him a lot

Cooper's career has been borne out of pain. He has reported stories and news coverage from many of the world's most dangerous places. He has been a witness the horrors of Bosnia and blood-shed of the Rwandian genocide, and has filmed numerous reports on human loss and suffering and against-the-odds tales of survival. Cooper seems to connect with the grieving, the shell-shocked, and the abandoned, as he was going through the same suffering, be it the citizens of loss in Southeast Asia or in his late father's former stomping grounds, New Orleans.

The coverage of the aftermath of Hurricane Katrina , tragedy faced by the American people that saw the anchor, live on CNN, confronting government authorities, demanding answers, thundering bureaucrats with unflinching questions, and crying out in agitation and frustration. This experience affected him so deeply that he began to come to terms with his own family's loss and how they have influenced him, both on and off the camera roll.

Elaborating on his philosophy as a TV and news anchor, Cooper has said, "I think the notion of traditional anchor is fading away, the all-knowing, all-seeing person who speaks from on high. I don't think the audience really buys that anymore. As a viewer, I know I don't buy it. I think you have to be yourself, and you have to be real and you have to admit what you don't know, and talk about what you do know, and talk about what you don't know as long as you say you don't know it. I tend to relate more to people on television who are just themselves, for good or for bad, than I do to someone who I believe is putting on some sort of persona. The anchorman on The Simpsons is a reasonable facsimile of some anchors that have that problem."

10 COMING OUT OF THE CLOSET

Anderson Cooper is openly gay. He is the second "Most Powerful Gay Men and Women in America" as ranked by Out Magazine in May 2007. The magazine also featured Cooper's face on the cover of its "Glass Closet" issue with the title: "Why the Stars Won't Come Out and Play". There was a lot of speculation about his sexuality since years. He chose to keep it private and always declined to discuss it publicly. He defended his decision not to discuss his private life, telling New York Magazine, "I understand why people might be interested. But I just don't talk about my personal life."

Cooper's confession of his sexual orientation had been

an open secret in TV circles since long, but it was a bold attempt on his part to announce it publicly. He is also among few TV personalities who have come out in the open in the recent years. He came to publicly admitting his homosexuality after same-sex marriage became legal in the state of New York.

His admission of his sexuality was published on the blog, "The Dish" by Daily Beast's Andrew Sullivan in July 2012. Cooper had revealed that he was gay via an email to Sullivan in response to an article by Entertainment Weekly on how gay public figures are increasingly coming out in more restrained ways than in the past. He wrote "The fact is, I'm gay, always have been, always will be, and I couldn't be any more happy, comfortable with myself, and proud."

He had intended to keep his sexuality private "for professional reasons" but had "begun to consider whether the unintended outcomes of maintaining his privacy outweigh personal and professional principle." As a news reporter and journalist, Cooper was happy keeping his personal life separate from professional since he's often reporting in areas where he might be targeted for being gay.

He however feels lucky to experience life as a gay man. The experience has him taught perspective, empathy and provided him a much better understanding of the world around him.

Hearing about the increasing incidences of gay bullying, made him realize that he need to make it clear where he stood. In his own words, "There continue to be far too many incidences of bullying of young people, as well as discrimination and violence against people of all ages, based on their sexual orientation, and I believe there is value in making clear where I stand". He was in support of Barack Obama's endorsement of gay marriage and considered it a great example to put an end to bullying.

He is a reserved person and likes a small amount of personal space. Although he still considers visibility as more important than preserving his privacy. When he was questioned on why his memoir did not address his sexual orientation, he justified the reason explaining the book focused on war, disasters, loss and survival and contained no other aspects of my life.

The fact that his long silence on his sexuality, had given some the impression that he was trying to hide something made it distressing for him. He feared he might be setting a bad example. In candid comments in an interview he said that he was not an activist, but he was a human being and he didn't want to give that up by being a journalist. He is proud of his orientation and does not feel uncomfortable, ashamed or even afraid. Not once regretting his decision he wrote, "I am also blessed far beyond having a great career. I love, and I am loved."

He came out with the truth to his mother when he was 21 years of age. In an interview to *CBS Sunday Morning,* he admits how he was open about it to friends in high school. The initial hesitation he felt was in confessing it to his mother. Back then there were rumors of his grandmother being a lesbian and it had upset his mother as a child.

Cooper knew deep down that his mother would be fine and remembered his mother invite gay friends in their house all the time. He recalls how he just went to her room one day and talked about it. She was very understanding and accepted the fact ultimately. On one such occasion in 1979 when Cooper asked her about a gay couple who were coming to dinner, she introduced them as a married couple. Cooper was luckier in this sense since parents in USA at that time were not as accepting of homosexuality as his mother was and wouldn't have seen gay couples like them as married.

Infact, he even revealed one of his childhood crushes during a guessing game on his daytime show Friday. He admitted to have a crush on actor Scott Baio. Baio has been a guest on Cooper's show, but Cooper confessed that he didn't have the courage to tell him that he was one of his childhood crushes.

10 PARTNER

Cooper has been in a relationship with French nightclub and gay bar owner Benjamin Maisani. Anderson's partner, French Maisani, runs nightclubs like the "Eastern Bloc", "Bedlam", "Atlas Social Club" and "LOVEGUN" in New York. He met Benjamin in 2009, and the two have been a couple ever since. Cooper had attended the launch of Maisani's

Atlas Social Club (in Hell's Kitchen).

Cooper had kept his relationship with Maisani fairly private. Even Maisani keeps a particularly low profile and was quoted by French Morning to have never wanted to be a celebrity. Recently in 2014, the couple bought the Rye House, a historic estate in Connecticut.

Anderson Cooper was encouraged by his mother, designer Gloria Vanderbilt to patch up his relationship with Maisani since they had to struggle a lot with their conflicting work schedules. She has also been encouraging him to adopt a child as she is desperate to see her son settled down. Cooper admitted that his mom wants him to have kids. That is something that she'd like to see and even Cooper would certainly love to have kids. Commenting on how having children was very much on his mind he said, "I love kids. Who knows? I work a lot, so I would have to kind of change my work schedule."

10 INHERITENCE

Gloria Vanderbilt is the heiress to one of America's greatest fortunes. Of her four sons, Anderson was considered to be the sole heir. However it has been established that although his mother inherited a fortune before making her own millions, Cooper will not acquire his inheritance. According to Cooper his mother made it very clear to him that there's no trust fund for him.

Despite the family's vast fortune, Cooper was determined to become financially self-dependent and self-reliant, the reason being that he does not believe in inheriting money. He is of the opinion that those who have inherited a lot of money have not themselves gone on to do things in their own life. "From the time I was growing up, if I felt that there was some pot of gold waiting for me, I don't know that I would've been so motivated."

Opposing strongly to inheriting money, Cooper has remarked he was against inheriting money because it's an initiative sucker and curse. He has no regrets about not receiving any part of his mother's $200 million fortune. In fact calling his mother the coolest person he knows, he is grateful that his mother always gave him an incentive to work. He is ever appreciative of her for instilling within him a great work ethic.

He himself wants to follow in her footsteps, should he become a father one day. He is a man who would want his children to start working early on and realise their sense of responsibility. He said, "If maybe I felt like they had a good sense of responsibility, maybe I would try to leave some money."

Cooper never expected to receive any of his mother's $200 million fortune from the beginning as admitted by him in an interview. Although he is exceptionally close to his mother he is insistent that he doesn't want her money. Not that he feels ashamed; he just doesn't want it to be portrayed in the wrong way. Having Cornelius Vanderbilt as ancestor one of the world's richest business magnates of the 1800s, he does not want to look like he has got everything the easy way. Cooper is a self-made man and does not want to depend on his mother's inheritance. Moreover, since his mother was not close to her family, his connection to the "Vanderbilt" family does not seem real to him.

He has the last name of his father writer Wyatt Cooper; he wanted to keep it that way. Being more like his dad, who grew up in really poor family in Mississippi, he believes in standing on his own feet.

10 ACCOMPLISHMENTS

The charming and famous journalist Anderson Cooper has had a terrific journey up till now and has been deservingly bestowed upon with quite a few awards. He is one among the hundreds of journalist worldwide who possess a reporting style with a personal tinge. At the beginning of his reporting career, as early as 1993, he won the Bronze Telly Award for his exceptional coverage of famine in Somalia.

This was followed by the 1997 Emmy Award by ATAS/NATAS for covering Princess Diana's funeral. In 2001, he won the GLAAD Media Award by Gay & Lesbian Alliance Against Defamation for the 20/20 Downtown: "High School Hero" – report on high school athlete Corey Johnson in the category of Outstanding TV Journalism. He was also given the Peabody Award in 2001 by Henry W. Grady College of Journalism and Mass Communication at the University of Georgia for his outstanding coverage of the aftermath of Hurricane Katrina in New Orleans.

Few years later in 2004, Cooper was awarded with the National Headliner Award by the Press Club of Atlantic City for the Anderson Cooper 360: "Wave of Destruction" – 2004 Indian Ocean earthquake and tsunami coverage. He was again honoured by 2 Emmy Award in 2006, one for Anderson Cooper 360: "Charity Hospital" in the category

Outstanding Feature Story in a Regularly Scheduled Newscast and the other for Anderson Cooper 360: "Starving in Plain Sight" in the category Outstanding Live Coverage of a Breaking News Story – Long Form.

The 2007 Emmy Awards gave Anderson Cooper 360 two nominations, the "Sago Mines" for Outstanding Live Coverage of a Breaking News Story – Long Form and the "High Rise Crash" for Outstanding Individual Achievement in a Craft: Lighting Direction & Scenic Design.

Cooper also has to his name the National Order of Honour and Merit by the Government of Haiti in 2010 for his Reporting on 2010 Haiti earthquake. In 2011, Anderson Cooper 360: "Haiti in Ruins" won an Emmy in the Outstanding Coverage of a Breaking News Story in a Regularly Scheduled Newscast category and in the same year the Anderson Cooper 360: "Crisis in Haiti" also won an Emmy award for Outstanding Live Coverage of a Current News Story – Long Form. He was again awarded the GLAAD Media Award by Gay & Lesbian Alliance against

Defamation in the category of the Vito Russo Award in 2013.

Apart from the above Cooper has also been honoured with the Silver Plaque from the Chicago International Film Festival for his report from Sarajevo on the Bosnian War. He also won a Bronze Award from the National Education Film and Video Festival for a report on political Islam.

He was Number 3 on Playgirl magazine's Sexiest Newscasters List in 2004. In second place was Fox News Channel's Sean Hannity and in first place was MSNBC's Keith Olbermann.

The Out Magazine in May 2007 ranked him Number 2 among "The Most Powerful Gay Men and Women in America". He was among the Top 10 men on Vanity Fair's international best-dressed list, which was published in the magazine's April 2004 issue. His name appeared again on the international best-dressed list in the magazine's September 2006 issue.

Cooper is a man who gives his time to many

important charitable causes. To name a few AIDS & HIV, Children, Civil Rights, Health, Human Rights, LGBT Support, Rape/Sexual Abuse are some of these. He has taken an active participation in supporting gay and lesbian issues publicly.

In April 2016, he also donated his speaking fee for his Norfolk Forum speech to retired SEAL Jimmy Hatch's charity Spike's K9 Fund. A Norfolk police dog named Kriger was killed in line of duty in a standoff with a man who'd barricaded himself in his house. Cooper saw a social media post about Hatch's new fundraising effort to buy 18 ballistic vests that will protect dogs in the Norfolk Police Department's entire K-9 unit. Cooper had interviewed Hatch in 2015 and decided to donate the speaking fee for the vests that cost about $2,200.

Anderson Cooper is also known to support various charitable organisations such as American Heart Association, American Stroke Association, Elton John AIDS Foundation, GLAAD, Hillsides and Robert F Kennedy

Memorial. With an annual income of approximately $11 million from CNN, he regularly donates book and appearance fees to charity. His CNN news show Anderson Cooper 360° has been donating million dollar earnings for several cancer charities.

Anderson Cooper is a man of character. Most people have faced ups and downs in life and no one is perfect. Cooper is a man who used the downs and his weakness in life to his advantage to shape out his career. With his remarkable reporting and going beyond the headlines style, the Silver Fox of CNN is a great source of inspiration for the young aspiring journalists and news reporters.

Crystal Reynolds

ABOUT THE AUTHOR

Crystal Reynolds is a writer from Detroit, Michigan with a passion for TV personalities. She paints in her free time and enjoys hiking with her two huskies.

Manufactured by Amazon.ca
Bolton, ON